e, and eat out their substance —

nd superior to the Civil power —

retended Legislation : — For Quartering large boo

the Inhabitants of these States : — For cutting

benefits of Trial by Jury : — For transporting us

in an Arbitrary government, and enlarging its Bou

way our Charters, abolishing our most valuable Laws

with power to legislate for us in all cases whatsoe

ravaged our Coasts, burnt our towns, and destroyed the

, already begun with circumstances of Cruelty & per

ens taken Captive on the high Seas to bear Arms

rections amongst us, and has endeavoured to bring

onditions. In every stage of these Oppressions

t is thus marked by every act which may define a Ty

time of attempts by their legislature to extend an unwar

justice and magnanimity, and we have conjured t

They too have been deaf to the voice of justice and

MY AMERICAN JOURNEY

From Colonies to Country

with George Washington

BY DEBORAH HEDSTROM

ILLUSTRATIONS BY SERGIO MARTINEZ

FROM COLONIES TO COUNTRY WITH GEORGE WASHINGTON

My American Journey Series published by Questar Publishers
© 1997 by Questar Publishers

Illustrations © 1997 by Sergio Martinez

International Standard Book Number: 1-57673-155-3

Design by D² DesignWorks

Printed in Mexico

For information:
Questar Publishers, Inc. - Post Office Box 1720 - Sisters, Oregon 97759

LIBRARY OF CONGRESS CATALOGING-IN-PUBLICATION DATA
Hedstrom, Debbie.
From colonies to country with George Washington / by Debbie Hedstrom.
p.   cm. — (My American journey ; 2)
Summary: A fictionalized account of the Revolution War,
told from the point of view of an aide to George Washington.
ISBN 1-57673-155-3 (alk. paper)
1. United States—History—Revolution, 1775-1783—Juvenile fiction.
2. Washington, George, 1732-1799—Juvenile fiction.
[1. United States—History—Revolution, 1775-1783—Fiction. 2. Washington, George, 1732-1799—Fiction.]
I. Title.   II. Series.
PZ7.H3566Fr 1997   96-38013
[Fic]—dc21   CIP
                                        AC

97 98 99 00 01 02 03 04 — 10 9 8 7 6 5 4 3 2 1

Foreword

He stares at us from every one-dollar bill, but we hardly notice. We already know he's George Washington, the first president of the United States.

But look again. His face appears serious and old, not heroic or adventuresome. So why did Americans two hundred years ago pick him to be their leader? What did he do? How did George Washington help the American colonies become a free country? This book will answer some of those questions.

The events, the battles, the men and women, the plots, and the timing—all these elements of our story are true. A little imagination filled in missing details such as exact words and gestures. Also, as in other My American Journey books, one fictional character has been added for fun. Ben Johnston, Washington's assistant aide, is not a real person.

However, the general did have a few aides-de-camp, including Alexander Hamilton.

Many reports, letters, and diaries were written during the Revolutionary War. Men in the militia wrote their families. Officers reported to other officers. Early newspapers told of battles. And wives kept diaries. Information taken from such actual records created during the Revolution were used to make up Ben's fictional report.

When you turn this page and enter Samuel Adams's parlor, you'll step into the beginning of a war—a war for your freedom. From the pounding hoofs of Paul Revere's horse to the clomp of the retreating British boots, you'll learn what George Washington really did during that long, desperate conflict, and you'll see why we call him "the Father of Our Country."

Introduction

I waited in Mr. Adams's dark, ornate parlor, nervously swaying from one foot to the other, wondering why the famous political leader had summoned me, a lad of only sixteen, at such an early hour. Suddenly brisk footsteps echoed in the hallway, and Samuel Adams, himself, stood in the doorway. Without so much as a "Good morning!" he launched into a hurried speech.

"Thank you for coming, Ben Johnston. No doubt you are wondering why I asked you to my home. Let me get right to the point. I have heard you have no love for English rule. Though young, you have spoken of freedom. If this is true, hear me out. If not, you had best leave now."

He raised one eyebrow then smiled briefly as I stood, unmoving. He nodded, recognizing my acceptance, then continued hurriedly.

"Since you have chosen to stay, I'll tell you plainly: I, Samuel Adams, am a patriot. I would rather that 999 out of 1,000 Americans fall in a war for liberty than see this country enslaved. King George cares not for us. He values only what he takes from our colonies. We must pay his taxes. We must feed and house his soldiers. We must serve in his navy. The king says we are his citizens, yet no Englishman in London is treated as we are. We don't even have a vote in Parliament! We have no say at all in governing our own affairs.

"This is intolerable and must be stopped! Already many people oppose the king. You yourself stood watch for the little 'tea party' in Boston's harbor. Other colonists died in the massacre of our townspeople. Many have joined me in the group we call Sons of Liberty.

"Even our women seek a free country. Recently a young Loyalist man went to a quilting bee and spoke against our First Continental Congress. The ladies didn't have tar or feathers, but they made do. They grabbed the man, stripped off his shirt, and poured molasses and flower pedals all over him!

"Though many Americans believe we can come to terms with the king, more and more agree with

Patrick Henry, who declared, 'Give me liberty or give me death.'

"War is coming. It has been six months since Congress sent the king our Declaration of Rights and Grievances. He has dismissed our claims. Our colonies will not stand for it. We will fight to become a free country, and you can help us by doing an important job.

"On May tenth a Second Continental Congress will meet to take action against the king. My cousin John Adams plans to nominate George Washington as 'commander in chief' of the army we raise. I'll be there to second the nomination. Washington is respected and believes in freedom. When he was only nineteen years old, he became a major in Virginia's militia and fought in the French and Indian War.

"As the leader of our army, this man and the events that occur around him will decide if we become a free country or stay enslaved as colonies.

"His activities, these historical events, must be recorded. Up until now Washington has kept his own diary. However, as our military commander, he will lack the time to continue this practice. Tasks of war will keep even his aides-de-camp from recording events. But I will recommend you as his assistant aide. In this position, you can keep an account of our fight for freedom.

"It is my understanding that you write and read well. This is enough. A journal of events need not be fancy, but it must be clear. Your young age is an advantage. People will say and do things in front of you that they would not do before an adult.

"But make no mistake; your job is dangerous. Youth will not stop British agents or the king's Loyalists from spotting your close tie to Washington. Don't be surprised if they seek to harm you or bribe you. Your best protection is your own sense of right and wrong.

"Above all else, help Washington. You have a reputation for being a hard worker. Keep it up as the general's assistant aide. Whether carrying messages for him or caring for his horse, do your best. But whenever you can, jot down the events that are occurring, the people he meets, the words spoken, and the actions taken. Send them to me whenever you find a way. God willing, one day they'll be read by free men and women.

"It's a fine thing you've agreed to do, lad. I bid you Godspeed and look forward to your first record of independence history."

SAMUEL ADAMS'S HOME
BOSTON, MASSACHUSETTS, APRIL 17, 1775

Chapter One

A SECRET MARCH

Cambridge, outside of Boston, July 2, 1775

Tomorrow General Washington takes charge of our troops outside of Boston, so I'm writing my first report. The Revolution didn't get started the way I expected. I guess I figured somebody would say, "Go!" and we'd all start fighting. But truth was, it began in secret.

Like you, Mr. Adams, the English knew war was coming. They tried to stop it before it started. They'd heard of our carts loaded with gunpowder and balls lumbering into Concord. Then they got word that you and John Hancock would be visiting in a friend's home in Lexington. Since only ten miles separated Lexington and Boston, the British sent secret orders to their commander in Boston, urging him to, "Organize a surprise attack: Arrest the rebel leaders Adams and Hancock. Proceed on to Concord. Capture or destroy all ammunition."

After you and Mr. Hancock knocked on your friend's door in Lexington, eight hundred British soldiers left Boston after dark. None talked, and all kept their rifles and powder horns quiet as they marched. They crossed the Charles River in boats and took an untraveled route through the marshes. Eight miles away, you and everyone else in Lexington went to sleep, not knowing the approaching danger.

But the patriots in Boston weren't deaf. The sound of hundreds of boots and creaking oars can only be kept so quiet! The British had barely shoved off from shore when two lantern lights appeared in the tower of a church and flashed a warning across the bay to our rebels in Charlestown.

William Dawes told me what happened next. "I made it out of Boston before the sentries got word to close off the city," he said. "I rode as fast as my horse could carry me on the dark road. Meanwhile, Paul Revere saw the signal lanterns and headed up the Medford Road. He hit Lexington before I did, shouting to everybody along the way, 'The British are coming!'"

"After warning our leaders of the danger, we headed for Concord. That's when we met Doc Prescott. He joined us, and it's a good thing he did!

"Revere was in the lead when the redcoats burst out of the bushes along the road. They surrounded him, and a minute later they got me too. But Doc's horse leaped away, and he avoided being captured. While the British soldiers questioned and threatened us, we kept hoping that Doc made it through. When we heard the church bells clanging, we sighed in relief."

Thanks to the daring ride of these brave men, the patriots were warned of the redcoats' approach. So when the British hit Lexington and started banging on doors, they found no leaders. When they entered Concord, they found no military stores. Their fast, eighteen-mile march was for nothing! Tired, hungry, and angry, they burned the courthouse. Then they got a big surprise.

"Look!" a private shouted.

Glancing through the clouds of smoke drifting up from the courthouse, the redcoats spotted four hundred angry minutemen gathered on the outskirts of the town. The British commander called a retreat.

Along every step of the redcoats' march back to Boston, a minuteman was hiding in the trees and brushes, ready to aim and fire at the British soldiers. It caused panic. Even when the redcoats were joined by more than a thousand soldiers from Boston, they didn't hold against the ambush of flying bullets. They ran, leaving their wounded behind. One of them later said, "The colonists seemed to have dropped from the clouds."

That day 273 redcoats never made it back to Boston, and everybody knew about the "secret" march.

We wanted to keep the British retreating—right back to their ships. But it wasn't easy because we couldn't just march into town. Boston is on an arm of land that juts into a bay that opens into the ocean. It's surrounded by hills, small towns, and fingers of ocean cutting into the mainland. So our militia set up a stronghold by Bunker Hill and waited for the British to attack.

Meanwhile, up north, our Colonels Ethan Allen and Benedict Arnold captured Fort Ticonderoga and Crown Point. When our militia outside Boston got word of the victories, they cheered until the hills echoed.

Then they saw a fleet of ships.

General William Howe had arrived from England with more troops. Now our men on the hill faced ten thousand trained and well-armed redcoats!

Howe took one look at our homespun- and buckskin-clothed army and shook his head. "These colonists stand no chance against his majesty's forces," he scoffed.

We proved him wrong. When his troops rushed our hill, they ran smack into deadly musket fire and retreated. Again they were ordered to attack. And again our bull's-eye shooting turned them around.

By now the British had lost hundreds of men, and many British officers wanted to go back into Boston. But General Howe couldn't bear defeat after all his boasting. "Charge!" he told his remaining men.

Again our fire mowed through their ranks, but then our men began to call to one another,

"I'm down to three balls and a bit of powder. I need more!"

When our last ammunition was spent, hand-to-hand fighting started. Outnumbered five to one, we retreated across an arm of the bay. We might have lost the battle, but now we knew we could defeat the king's soldiers.

A few weeks later our Second Congress made George Washington commander in chief of the army. He didn't take the job right off, saying he wasn't sure if he could do it. Only after talking with his wife, Martha, did he finally accept it as a kind of destiny. But he refused to be paid. "I do not wish to make a profit. My expenses is all I desire."

As his new assistant aide, I heard it all, including the reports General Washington got about Lexington, Concord, Ticonderoga, and Bunker Hill. Tomorrow we join our troops outside Boston. The general is going to take command of them.

It's late, and I should get some sleep, but I am so excited. The Revolution has really started. Tomorrow we'll show those redcoats a thing or two!

Chapter Two

A DEATH PLOT

New York, June 1776

I'm breathing a sigh of relief as I write out this report. I guess I thought fighting redcoats would be all excitement and glory. It's not. I started seeing that from the first moment we got to our camp outside of Boston.

It was a mess! Makeshift tents and lean-tos dotted the field. The troops lacked everything—uniforms, weapons, ammunition, and supplies. They also didn't take to working together! Everyone wanted to elect his own officers, be loyal to his state, and leave the army when he pleased. General Washington had to settle squabbles, punish unruly officers, drill the men, and grant leave to those worrying about their crops. If he didn't already have gray hair, he surely would have gotten it then!

He kept his aide-de-camp, Alexander Hamilton, and me busy running messages: "Require supplies immediately." "Not enough men. Enlistments too short." "Paymaster without money. Credit used up. Must have funds."

Being a new government, Congress didn't have money. Since no colonist wanted to pay taxes, the only way Congress could get money was to make some! It got Paul Revere to print up a bunch. The trouble is, folks don't trust the paper dollars. They prefer gold. As for the British, they call our tender "pasteboard money" because it's stiff and thick.

In spite of these problems, Washington kept the British shut up in Boston. But he couldn't attack without gunpowder and balls. As one man said, "If the English knew we only had eight shots per man, they'd scatter us from here to the Allegheny Mountains!"

While we were stuck waiting for ammunition, our militia up north invaded Canada. Everybody had felt sure Canada would want to join our Revolution. But the Canadians weren't willing to help us, so Congress decided we should attack

them. That's when Colonels Allen and Arnold, along with General Montgomery, headed north.

Then one dark day in January a runner came in, all breathless, and blurted out, "The invasion of Canada has failed! Colonel Allen has surrendered, and General Montgomery has been killed!"

Later another messenger arrived. "The English fleet just burned Port Falmouth."

Then came news that made us angry and fearful at the same time. King George had hired twenty thousand German soldiers—Hessian mercenaries—to arrive next spring. "Ain't nobody going to be safe," one sergeant said. "Man or woman, young or old, soldier or settler—them professional soldiers kill 'em all."

That night the general talked to his officers. "By this brutal act of hiring Hessians, King George ends all chances of us reconciling with England. He makes it clear he doesn't want free Englishmen in his colonies; he wants slaves. Now we fight, not only to keep our rights, we fight to become a free country!"

I guess a lot of folks felt the same way. A group of them from up north hauled cannons and ammunition down to us. Using horses and sleds, they pulled the heavy guns through deep snow. They were fearful and exhausted when they arrived, but they gave us firepower.

A lot of this support is due to the pamphlet called "Common Sense" written by Thomas Paine. More than 500,000 copies have been sold! Everywhere people are reading about why we needed to break away from England. Now more men have started enlisting in the army.

With men, guns, and some ammunition, General Washington went after Boston. In March, the last redcoats left by ship. When they sailed out of the bay, the people cheered. But the general and Congress knew the mercenaries were yet to come. "Defend New York," our new orders said.

We marched into the city, singing "Yankee Doodle." Somebody in camp changed the words in the old jig to fit our army. But there were only eight thousand of us there to sing. Many of the Massachusetts militia had left. I heard one say, "We fought and won our town back. Let them New Yorkers fight to defend their own city."

Many did, but New York is on a group of islands, with even more places to defend than Boston. Our troops have to patrol the Hudson and East Rivers and the bridges as well as the islands. There just aren't enough of them. Staten Island couldn't be adequately guarded. Talking to Alex Hamilton, General Washington said, "Howe will float right in to the middle of us, and we cannot do one thing to stop him."

That's exactly what happened, but we did try and stop it with a new invention. A guy named Bushnell invented a battle boat that goes underwater. It's called a submarine. Washington sent it into the harbor when the British fleet appeared. "Bomb the flagship," he told the sergeant piloting it.

When the bomb went off, every redcoat in the fleet set to scurrying around. Even General Howe was yelling orders about manning the guns and getting out repair crews. But after the smoke cleared, everyone found out the bomb didn't even dent the copper-covered hull of the ship! Still, it sure scared them British.

I knew the General took it hard when we failed to stop the British. He kept slapping his riding whip against his leg, which isn't like him. The general is real proper about polite behavior. Drumming fingers, humming, or making idle noises in front of people—like the whop, whop of his whip—just isn't something he normally does.

Now when we look westward across the Hudson River toward New Jersey, we see a forest of masts—the British fleet.

I ended up in the middle of what happened next. I'm just glad I'm sighing with relief instead of grieving over the general's death.

When we marched into New York earlier this summer, its royal governor took refuge on Howe's ship, but he kept in touch with colonist friends on shore who were still loyal to the king. Together, they hatched a plot to blow up our ammunitions and murder General Washington! The mayor of the city joined the conspiracy, bribing one of the general's own guards to help in the monstrous plot.

The traitor guard started asking me a lot of questions. I answered a few but got to thinking that talking about the general wasn't right. I asked Hamilton. He agreed and did some poking around. In no time the plot became known. They arrested the mayor and hanged the guard. But it makes me wonder what else this war will bring. The plotters weren't Germans or even redcoats. They were colonists, still loyal to the king.

Chapter Three

OUTWITTED

Morristown, New Jersey, January 10, 1777

What a way to end the year! I think every one of us would give his life for General Washington right now. What he did during the last week of 1776 came just short of a miracle. But we needed it. Things had begun to look like we would lose our war for freedom.

At first things went well after exposing the plot to kill the general. The murder attempt came to be called the "Tryon Plot." It put Loyalists in a bad light. After the plot was exposed, more colonists took bolder stands against the British. When English ships sailed into Charleston, South Carolina, southerners put up a log-and-sand fort on an island just offshore. Their cannon fire drove off the ships, and deep tides and mosquitoes took care of the redcoats who tried to land. In the end, the British headed back to New York.

About that time, word came of the Declaration of Independence written by Thomas Jefferson and Benjamin Franklin. Colony after colony accepted it. When New York did, a bunch of soldiers celebrated by tearing down a bronze statue of King George. "Hey, I got an idea," one of them yelled. "Lets give ol' George back his statue bit by bit. We can melt this down and cast it into bullets!"

A few days later, more ships arrived from England. Their commander came with an offer to pardon us. He didn't send it to Congress because that would mean recognizing our government. Instead he sent it to General Washington. It made me proud to watch my commander. He refused the letter, saying, "I am a Virginia landholder and an American citizen. I have no authority to deal with a royal commissioner."

When the underhanded offer failed, the red-coats gathered in force. The Hessians arrived, along with more troops from England. Then the ones who had been defeated down in Charleston showed up.

General Howe now had twenty-five thousand soldiers! Meanwhile, recruits from around New York gave us eighteen thousand troops. But our army wasn't made up of well-trained soldiers; we were farmers, blacksmiths, shopkeepers, and the like. Outnumbered and untrained, we faced the military might of England.

Battle after battle took place. We lost ground. The general barely avoided getting his forces trapped by making a daring river crossing. Then Fort Washington fell. Looking on from across the river, the general stood attention straight as our forces surrendered.

None of us were prepared for what happened next. When our men laid down their rifles, the mercenaries opened fire on them.

I couldn't look. Turning away, I saw the general. It was as if all the hurt of this war started sliding down his cheeks. I'd never seen a man cry like that.

But the hurting wasn't over. When Washington ordered General Lee to bring his forces into battle, he ignored the command. As a result we lost. Redcoats chased us clean across the state of New Jersey until we crossed the Delaware River into Pennsylvania.

Lee blamed the loss of New York and New Jersey on Washington. He had the brass to suggest that if he was made dictator for one week, he could do great things. Bah!

On the run and losing ground, we looked like a lost cause to Howe. He left four thousand mercenaries to wipe us out while he headed north to take Newport. That's when Washington showed the British that Americans don't quit. That's when we learned we had a commander worth dying for.

It was Christmas, and a snowstorm blasted both sides of the Delaware River. Watching from Pennsylvania, Washington knew the enemy on the other side of the river would be drinking and celebrating in the warm houses of Trenton, trusting the storm more than sentries to guard them. We learned later that their German commander offered a holiday toast to "the Country Clown, General Washington."

While the redcoats toasted, Washington prepared to attack. Dividing his forces, he sent his officers up and down the river to cross while he took the middle. Huge chunks of ice bobbed in the stormy waves. The general got local boats and fishermen to help, but the other officers scattered along the river sent word, "Our division cannot make it across."

With only twenty-five hundred men, Washington did not stop. He led us across the dangerous river, and then we marched nine miles in blinding snow and sleet. When we attacked Trenton, the British surrendered after losing many men, including the commander who underestimated General Washington.

A soon as Howe heard that his mop-up forces had been defeated, he sent reinforcements to "run down the old fox and bag him in the morning." It didn't work. Joined by our other divisions, now across the river, Washington attacked again but not like anyone expected. He left fires burning and marched us around Howe's forces. We took out the ammunition stores behind them, causing panic.

In three weeks Washington turned the war around. We regained all the land lost except New York City. We set up camp in Morristown, locking in the English.

We've gone from expecting failure to the cheers of victory. By the light of our campfires, we tell tales of our amazing battles. Every day more men join us. It is a good scene to look upon after so much fighting. However, I sense that the general is ill at ease. His men shiver, and their cooking pots aren't full.

Chapter Four
A FLAG FLIES

Valley Forge, December 20, 1777

This war isn't what I expected. Most of the time it seems as if nobody gets anywhere. We keep fighting over the same ground. All this year, we've been dug in outside New York. Now we're wintering in Valley Forge, just a few miles from where we fought the battle of Trenton last December!

We've built huts, but the lack of food, shoes, clothes, and blankets makes the winter cold hardly bearable. Every day men desert and head back to their farms. Washington got Congress to establish a war-long enlistment, but many don't take to the orders.

The general stays strong before the men, encouraging them and paying for supplies even though Congress still hasn't covered any of his expenses. Nothing seems to stop his strength of purpose. But today I realized it isn't easy for him either.

A runner came in with information the general wanted, so I went looking for him.

I scouted the camp and then headed through some woods to see if he'd returned to headquarters. Coming to an old oak grove, I heard a voice. Taking a few steps closer, I saw the general. He was kneeling in the snow and praying. I didn't stick around, thinking of his privacy, but I couldn't help hearing him say, "Oh Lord, I need wisdom."

It made me do some thinking. Winning or losing battles, the general carries a load. All year long he's been tackling the British, dealing with changes from Congress, or handling problems among his officers. It's been just one thing after another.

It started when Howe kept trying to break out of New York. Somehow we always drove his troops back. One captured redcoat said folks in Europe are calling Washington "the American Fabius."

When I asked about Fabius, he said, "He com-

manded Rome's army before it became an empire. He fought large forces with only a few troops, becoming a master of delaying tactics and wearing the enemy down."

It's a good name for the general. He says, "We cannot defeat the British. We must wear them down, harass them at every point, and never let our army be captured."

While Washington kept Howe in New York, news of other battles arrived regularly but sometimes weeks after they happened. Depending on how far the messenger must come, it can be three weeks before news gets to us!

In June, it took me only three days to make it to Boston with a message. While there, I saw John Paul Jones and his ship, the Ranger. Some of the crew members were sending up a flag. "What's going on?" I asked.

"We got us a new flag to fly from the mast," one sailor answered. "Congress had a widow named Betsy Ross put together a new one, seeing as how we're a new country."

When the wind caught the material and straightened it out, I saw red and white stripes and a blue corner box holding a circle of thirteen stars. It brought a lump to my throat. We might be thirteen colonies, but we were fighting to become one

country, and it made me proud to take part in it. I had the honor of carrying one of the new flags back to Morristown. But that wasn't all I brought back.

A Frenchman named (I hope I get this right) Marie Joseph Paul Yves Roch Gilbert du Motier, marquis de Lafayette came with me too. He's not much older than I am, but he crossed the Atlantic with a ship full of supplies for us. Right off he gave clothes and rifles to barefooted soldiers he saw dressed in rags. That's why Congress made him a major general.

At first Washington wasn't too happy about having such a young officer. But when I brought the Frenchman in to meet him, I could tell they hit it off. They get closer every day. It amazes me that this rich man even sleeps in muddy fields when Washington does. Once the marquis told me, "General Washington is my *beau idéal*. I wish to be like him."

He got his chance. Not long after he joined us, Howe broke out of New York. He marched toward our capital, Philadelphia. At the same time, another bunch of redcoats came out of Canada to take control of the Hudson River. Washington led us against Howe, and Congress put General Gates in charge up north.

General Washington had his hands full, outmaneuvering the English troops. For months we marched up one hill and down another. Always we got the best defensive position to stop the British. Finally Howe went back to New York.

News coming down from the north started bad but then got better. The British won some battles, using Indian allies and German mercenaries. The brutal fighters attacked settlers and families, as well as our soldiers. One messenger told us, "Folks up north are riled. More are joining the army every day. Right now we outnumber them murderers. And that don't count all the settlers who fire at redcoats on sight."

Outside New York, we all thought Howe would send help to his forces on the Hudson River. He didn't! He went after Philadelphia again! Much as it surprised us, it must have made his northern generals feel downright sick. Still they might have escaped, except for Benedict Arnold. General Gates wouldn't attack even though we outnumbered the enemy. When Arnold objected, Gates put him behind the battle line. Arnold watched the British slipping away and couldn't take it. He jumped on his horse and led his men into battle. Soon all our troops were fighting. On October 17 the British surrendered almost six thousand soldiers! Their military supplies sure boosted our slim stores.

Meanwhile down by the capital, we needed help. Howe's troops were getting past us.

Washington sent a runner with orders for Gates to send reinforcements. He ignored the order, saying, "I answer only to Congress."

Even without help, we came within a hairsbreadth of defeating Howe. But our troops lacked experience, and the communication between our officers got mixed up. In the end the British took Philadelphia. So right now they're sitting out winter in the comfort of a town while we shiver here at Valley Forge.

Besides this hardship, there's still the problem with Gates. He wants to be commander in chief and won't support the general. Also, Congress reorganized the supply office over Washington's objection. Now barrels of shoes and supplies sit on roadsides, without teams or men to haul them here. Many in our army go barefooted; they left blood on the snow as they marched here.

The general's wife is here, doing all she can to help. All of us admire her, but we sure don't admire the people living nearby. For them the war just seems like a chance to get rich. Farmers take their produce and stock into the capital, selling to the British who can pay in gold. Meanwhile our men starve.

General Washington's men are cold and hungry. Gates is trying to discredit him in Congress. I don't know how he keeps going. Maybe it's the praying?

Chapter Five
ATTACKS FROM INSIDE AND OUT

West Point, New York, January 15, 1779

A runner just hit camp. The British captured Savannah sixteen days ago! A dark mood has overtaken us. No sooner had we pushed most of the redcoats out of the north, and they struck the south. It made us feel like getting past last year's troubles didn't matter much.

But I know that's not true.

General Washington still commands us. Gates and his supporters almost succeeded in getting rid of him, though. They told Congress the general's mistakes cost us Philadelphia. Of course, no one mentioned the lack of reinforcements! Washington knew his job might end. He wrote Patrick Henry, "As long as the cause of independence goes forward, I don't care if I or another man does it."

But others did care, knowing the general's honor. In the end, some of Gates's own letters exposed him. Though it cleared the general, he still feels concerned for his officers. Excellent men such as Colonel Arnold get overlooked for promotion while lesser men get commands.

Added to the political fuss, our army was suffering at Valley Forge. For months we wondered if we'd ever feel warm or full again. But no one got to sit and stew about it. Baron Friedrich von Steuben arrived from Germany and kept us busy learning military order.

Our ragged appearance didn't bother the baron. He set to work with a passion. I heard one soldier tell another, "He ain't like them other officers who think it's beneath them to join us on the drill field."

"Yeah," the other replied. "He gets right in among us, showing how to do stuff. It don't matter that he doesn't speak like us, either."

"That's for sure. When he says, 'Achtung!' no interpreter needs to tell me to click my heels together and stand straight."

We needed every bit of the baron's training

when spring came. Washington got word that Howe had resigned, and a General Clinton had taken his place. Right off, the new British commander left Philadelphia and started marching his men back to New York. In record time fifteen thousand of us were hotfooting it after them.

General Washington wanted to fight, but the English kept dodging us. So we split up and forced them into battle at Monmouth, New Jersey. Trouble was, we didn't plan on General Lee letting us down!

He'd been captured in Boston but freed in a prisoner exchange. As we approached Monmouth, Washington put him in charge of a support attack. At a critical point when Lee needed to bring his men into the battle, he retreated. And he ordered other officers to do the same! It didn't make sense, so Lafayette sent a runner to Washington.

The private barely got his message out when the general wheeled his horse and raced back. I'd never seen him so angry. I could barely keep up with him. "What is the meaning of this, sir?" he shouted at Lee after reaching his position.

The officer didn't answered. He just trembled.

"I desire to know the meaning of this disorder and confusion!" Washington demanded again.

Then Lee got mad. "The American troops would not stand the British bayonets."

"You poltroon! Have you ever tried them?" Washington snapped. Reigning his mount with some of the finest horsemanship I'd ever seen, Washington halted the retreat and restored order.

With our forces called back into the battle, the men fought bravely. I should say men and women! Mary Hays, now better known as "Molly Pitcher," carried water to her husband, a cannoneer, and to other soldiers. Her man died during Lee's retreat.

"When she saw him dead, she took over his cannon," a soldier told me. "Over and over she loaded and fired the big gun. No one could have done a better job!"

After the battle, the general heard about Molly. He went to see her and asked, "Were you not afraid?"

"Of course, sir," she answered. "But the job needed doing. I was alive, and my John wasn't."

Despite our hard fighting, Clinton made it to New York. Both sides lost a lot of men. After setting up camp outside the city, the general sent a letter to Congress, putting Lee up for treason. There's talk that Lee became a turncoat when he was captured. I don't know about that, but retreating made him look mighty bad.

The next thing we knew, we were right back where we were in '76—outside New York. Only this time we were supposed to attack. Our plans called for cannon fire from ships promised by France. But when they arrived, things didn't go well.

Hearing about the approaching French fleet, the British ships hightailed it to different ports. Congress developed a second plan to attack the British in Rhode Island. But our northern troops got delayed, and a storm hit the French. When it ended, their boats could only limp into Boston for repairs.

Washington met with his officers and Congress to figure out what to do next. "We dare not let Clinton break out of New York," he told them. "Yet we are needed in so many other places."

As if to prove the general's words, a runner from the west arrived with a letter from Colonel George Rogers Clark. Opening his leather pouch, the messenger took out the paper and read, "My militia took three towns. British rule has been broken, but Loyalists with their Indian allies continue to attack settlements. Mohawk Chief Joseph Brant massacred all residents in Cherry Valley, New York. Senecas killed all in the Wyoming Valley of Pennsylvania."

The word "massacre" brought the general's head straight up. He asked to see the message and read it himself. When finished, he looked at the runner. "Tell me what you know of Colonel Clark."

"George Clark knows the woods, sir. He's been a scout, but by trade, he's a surveyor. As for the man himself, he's got staying power. You can count on him."

"And this Brant?" asked Washington.

"Folks are saying he's the devil himself. But truth is, he's educated and a right faithful Episcopalian. They say he's the son of Sir William Johnson, the Indian agent some of the Indians called "the Great White Father." Trouble is, he fights like a Mohawk chief!"

The general turned to Hamilton and me. "Ben, get this man some food. Alex, prepare an answer for Colonel Clark. Tell him that help to defeat the Indians will arrive in the spring."

Remembering that Clark broke the British hold out west doesn't lift the dark mood caused by Savannah's defeat. Our General Robert Howe surrendered a thousand American soldiers and all their supplies. Can we recover from this loss? How can we stop the redcoats from taking the other southern colonies?

Chapter Six

DON'T TREAD ON ME

Morristown, New Jersey, December 10, 1779

I don't want to write this report. Conditions couldn't be worse. For a year our troops defended the hills around New York while the French fleet took off for the West Indies. Our men have stopped every one of Clinton's efforts to escape the city, but we see no real progress. The British are in the same place as last year, only their clothes, shoes, and hearts are more ragged.

It didn't help when Congress issued another twenty-three million dollars in paper money. Nobody wants the stuff, so we can't buy what we need. Things are so bad that every night men disappear into the darkness. The desertion reduces our strength and makes things rougher for the general. Already he must pick and choose where to send men. Help is needed all over the colonies, but he can only support the most vital spots.

The camp's low morale isn't helped by most of the news reaching us. More cities in Georgia have been captured, and redcoats control most of the south. There is raiding and burning in Virginia. Worst of all, the entire navy Congress put together got trapped in Maine and was blown out of the water.

No matter how bad things look, a person can't help but admire General Washington. He doesn't give in to hard times. He is always our disciplined and proper commander in chief. Once he told me, "Ben, without military order we are doomed. The men must drill. They must maintain the camp. We must keep discipline."

To offset the bad news coming in, the general got men to read aloud the writings of Thomas Paine. They're real inspiring. I remember one line said, "These are the times that try men's souls."

Washington also made sure his men knew of every victory, no matter how small. Like town criers, men went through the camp yelling out any good news. "South Carolina turns back the

redcoats." "Spain declares war on England." "British forces have been run out of New Jersey."

In September a message caused Washington to nod his head with pleasure. Perhaps the news of massacres would end now. The troops he'd sent to Clark defeated the six Indian nations allied with England.

"Was Brant captured or killed?" the general asked the runner.

"No, sir. He escaped."

The general's brow furrowed. "Until we capture or kill this man or the war ends, he will be a threat to our settlers."

Another messenger set the men to cheering. John Paul Jones had captured a forty-four-gun British frigate! Men gathered around the runner, asking questions and wanting more news. "What happened?" "How'd he do it?"

The runner proved to be a good storyteller. "Jones sent the Ranger back home when the French gave him a battered old ship. The clumsy vessel couldn't turn on a wave to save itself. But Jones outfitted it with thirty-two rusty cannons and renamed it Bonhomme Richard after Ben Franklin's wise character, Poor Richard. Then he took to the sea with the most motley lot of vessels that ever made up a naval squadron. They raided the English coast and took a good bit of loot, but the French commanders sailing the other ships refused to obey him. In the end, he sailed alone, with the stars and stripes waving above his own rattlesnake flag. He sure proved the words written under that serpent: Don't tread on me.'"

As the runner talked, more and more men stopped to hear him. "While sailing alone, Jones came upon the Serapis. This British ship was a beauty and could outmaneuver Jones's ship sailing backward. As the two vessels faced each other, cannon fire filled the air. For three hours they blew holes in one another, with Jones's old tub getting the worst of it. That's when the British commander asked if Jones wanted to surrender. He yelled out, 'I have not yet begun to fight!'

"Captain Jones was waiting for the right moment to run the Bonhomme Richard in close. Then he lashed the ships together, and hand-to-hand fighting started. Hardly a man fought without wounds, and sweat and blood streaked every face. Only dogged determination left the Americans

standing when a well-thrown grenade touched off a row of British cartridges. Moments later the British captain surrendered."

"What happened to Jones's ship?" one of our soldiers asked.

"It sank the next morning despite efforts to save it. But it was a glorious day when Jones sailed to France in the Serapis."

For days men talked of the sea battle. But the cold and hunger of this winter eventually silenced the storytelling. Then I got wind of mutiny.

A couple of evenings ago, I took orders to a captain's tent. The freezing wind went right through the blanket wrapped around me, so I ducked behind a hut to get out of it. Old-timers say it's the coldest winter in a hundred years, and that night I believed it!

I was shivering in the shadows when two men walked by. They didn't see me and kept talking. "I tell you I won't take much more of this. If Washington can't get what we need, I say we take it," one said.

"Careful what you say, man. You're talking mutiny," the other replied.

"Call it what you will. Trouble is brewing, and unless supplies get here soon, I'm going to help it boil over."

Chapter Seven

A FOX IN THE HENHOUSE

Morristown, New Jersey, February 1, 1781

What a New Year's gift we received! We couldn't touch it, and it didn't have wrapping, but we sure felt it! After endless months of no progress in the north or south, General Greene is breaking Cornwallis's stranglehold on our southern colonies! A lot of the credit for Greene's being able to do it belongs to a "fox"!

"The Swamp Fox," General Francis Marion, started fighting for independence right after Lexington and Concord. He was part of the ragtag army in South Carolina that had sent the British retreating back to New York in '76. He was also there earlier this year when thirteen thousand more redcoats arrived.

One by one Marion had watched the southern commanders selected by the Congress fail: Robert Howe, defeated at Savannah; Benjamin Lincoln, defeated at Charleston; Horatio Gates, defeated at Camden. Only Marion's small band of volunteers remained to resist the invading army. That's when he took to the swamps.

He didn't have enough men to fight the British head-on, so he picked little targets.

Sometimes he attacked with thirty men, other times with three hundred. He destroyed camps, freed American prisoners, and attacked lagging regiments. Then he'd dash into the swamps, always letting the British know they didn't control all the south.

Try as they might, the redcoats couldn't find him in the tangle of southern swamplands. That's when they took to calling him the "Swamp Fox." They even put the butcher, Colonel Tarleton, after him. To be captured by this British colonel meant you'd die whether you surrendered or not!

One day Tarleton chased Colonel Marion for seven hours through thirty miles of swamp. He never got him! Finally he went after Colonel

Sumter, another hit-and-run fighter. He told his men, "We'll get the Gamecock, but as for this Swamp Fox, the devil himself could not catch him!"

News of the Swamp Fox's successful attacks has brought much-needed cheers to our camp here at West Point. The problems of last year have not gone away. They've worsened. Congress refused to listen to General Washington. He asked for Greene to be put in charge of our southern forces, but Congress picked their favorites instead, Lincoln and Gates. They tried, but between them, these two officers surrendered more than eight thousand American soldiers!

The supply problems got worse too. It kept taking more and more of our paper money to buy stuff. At one point, it took $1,575, or four months of a soldier's pay, to buy one barrel of flour! That's when the mutiny happened.

A Pennsylvania regiment loaded up their rifles and demanded full rations and immediate payment of salaries. When word of the mutiny reached headquarters, Hamilton told me, "Washington won't give in to the demands. Every man in camp suffers, not just these few. Though what they ask is right, to give in to their threats would only open the door to more mutiny."

The general's aide was right, and the men finally realized what they were doing was wrong. But later, when another mutiny arose among soldiers from New Jersey, Washington had to order up the Massachusetts regulars to punish the rebellious troops. Washington told the Massachusetts captain, "Mutiny will destroy any chance for independence. I want these men stopped now and their leaders arrested."

Ordering his own men punished went hard with the general, but he was about to face something even more difficult: ordering Benedict Arnold's arrest for treason!

It happened right after Washington and Lafayette had returned from having breakfast at Arnold's house! When they got back to headquarters in fine spirits, Alex Hamilton and I hated showing him the message. Finally Alex handed him the paper, and I said, "Sir, a courier just arrived with this. He told us a guard took it from a Loyalist traveling to New York."

Washington took the paper and opened it. Right off, I could tell he recognized the handwriting of his trusted officer. The note was addressed to Sir Henry Clinton, commander of the British forces, and it was signed by Arnold himself. As the general read the turncoat's directions telling Clinton how he could take our camp at West Point, it seemed his shoulders took on the weight of a thousand pounds. Benedict Arnold was a traitor!

The general went outside and ordered Arnold's arrest. I could almost imagine his thoughts. Arnold was passed over for promotion. He married a beautiful young woman from a Loyalist family. But treason?

Inside, Lafayette spoke to me. "This explains why Benedict left his home early this morning after getting a message. It must have told him of the courier's arrest."

Just then the door opened, and the general entered. Tears ran down his face. His voice broke as he said, "Arnold has fled to the British. Whom can we trust now?"

Thank God, things got better after that blow!

More than six thousand French troops landed in Rhode Island! British ships have blocked them in for now. But after winter, their strength will add to ours.

Also, Congress has finally realized its favorite officers weren't getting the job done down south. They let Washington put General Nathanael Greene in charge. He took up the Swamp Fox's ways. Reorganizing what was left of the army, he started attacking and running. He's living off the countryside and pushing back at ol' Cornwallis.

New hope fills the men. Surely now we will win our freedom. Lord, please let it be so.

Chapter Eight
AN UNEXPECTED MOVE

New York, November 1783

For five months in early 1981 my hopes fizzled like wet gunpowder. Then the French troops broke out of Rhode Island.

It took some doing, but General Washington met with their commander, Colonel Rochambeau. Both had to travel to Connecticut for their meeting. While Rochambeau bumped there in a rickety coach, the general rode with the worry of not having enough money to pay the innkeeper's bill. But that's when they got the idea of an unexpected move.

The general came back to camp thinking about it but had to put the idea on hold. News of Benedict Arnold arrived. "He's joined the British and is raiding in Virginia."

The lines around General Washington's eyes and mouth straightened liked soldiers coming to attention. "Tell Colonels von Steuben and Lafayette I want to see them."

When the two men arrived, the general told them of the traitor's raids. "Take your troops and stop him. This man has brought enough darkness to our country."

Next came some good news. The general learned that Greene had Cornwallis moving toward the coast. The news brought back the idea of an unexpected move. The British were sure we'd attack New York. What if we went south and boxed in Cornwallis?

"Ben," General Washington said to me, "information needs to be leaked to the British. I want them to think we're going after New York. See to it, will you, lad? And now send in my officers. We're going down to Chesapeake Bay!"

By the time the English figured out Washington wasn't moving just to lure them out of New York so he could attack it, Cornwallis was looking down musket barrels on every side. No English help could

arrive in time. On October 19, 1781, Cornwallis surrendered at Yorktown, Virginia.

American and French soldiers lined the road when the defeated redcoats marched out of Yorktown. Washington ordered no cheering. "I would have the British treated with the same respect that we would want," he said.

While praising his troops after the surrender, a captain told General Washington about a kid. "He started fighting in Savannah when he was just thirteen years old, sir," the man said. "His ma was widowed but took care of our captured men. She died of prison fever. He lost both his brothers too. One fell in battle while the other got smallpox in a British prison camp. The boy was also captured and carries the scar to prove it. When told to shine a redcoat's boots, he refused. The officer struck the boy's arm with his sword, cutting it to the bone."

The general asked to meet the boy who'd given so much for our country. "What's your name, son?"

"Andy Jackson, sir. I mean Andrew Jackson."

In spite of our success, Washington knew the war wasn't over. We returned to New York and set up camp outside it. We'd only been there a month when the general got a letter from a Colonel Nicola that really upset him. Nicola suggested that Washington use his army to take control of the country. "Make yourself king or dictator," Nicola wrote.

The general answered the colonel's letter using big words, but basically he told the guy his proposal made him sick. Then he added, "I am at a loss to understand what part of my conduct encouraged you to ask me to carry out the greatest mischief that can befall my country."

I know people don't get offered a crown every day. But anybody who'd seen the general spend his own money, sleep in mud, and put up with problems by the bucketful would know he wasn't after power. He believes in our country's right to rule itself.

Most everyone who fought for the general thinks the same way. Why, just a few months ago we found a twenty-two-year-old girl who did. She wanted a free country so much, she dressed like a boy and enlisted in Washington's army under a fake name, Robert Shurtliff.

She fought in the skirmishes after Yorktown. Her small size made the other soldiers think she was only fourteen or fifteen. They called her Bobby but sometimes teased her with the nickname "Blooming Boy." Still she marched every mile they did, carried her gear, and shivered in the cold until a redcoat's bullet hit her leg.

She needed a doctor, but getting help would mean being discovered. So she dug the bullet out herself and bandaged her leg as best she could. But it didn't heal. Sick with fever, she secretly left her post and made it to a small-town doctor. He found out her secret when she fell into a coma.

Under the care of the doctor and his wife, "Robert" got better. When she heard Ben Franklin was talking peace with England, she knew she had to clear "deserter" from her record. Dressed in a pretty pink dress, she came before her captain. The men she'd fought with couldn't believe her words. "I am Robert Shurtliff," she said. "I mean . . . well . . . really I'm Deborah Samson. I pretended to be a boy so I could fight."

Thousands of others besides Deborah sacrificed to fight in our war for freedom, and it paid off.

Though King George hung on like a bulldog with lockjaw, he lost. On April 18, 1783, exactly eight years from the day the first shots were fired in Concord, the peace treaty was announced.

On November 23 the British left New York, and we marched in, looking mighty ragged. But it didn't matter to the people. I heard one tell another, "These are our troops. I admire and glory in them more because they are weather-beaten and forlorn."

A lot of our soldiers had already gone home when we moved into New York. Today the general left, and finishing this report is my last job. When first asked to write these reports, I really didn't see their value. They were just one more job to get done. But then I met Washington, Captain Jones, the Swamp Fox, Colonel Clark, Andy Jackson, and Deborah Sampson. Now I'm glad you asked me to do this job, Mr. Adams.

So many gave so much to turn our colonies into a country. It cost more than I ever dreamed. Those who paid the price need to be remembered. Otherwise how will Americans know that their freedom isn't a light thing? It cost blood, tears, sacrifice, and lives.

Epilogue

A CLOSING NOTE

New York City, Federal Hall, May 2, 1789

Last night my second cousin, Samuel Adams, stopped by and gave me these reports. He told me, "Since you and George Washington just became our country's first president and vice president, I place these in your care."

It intrigued me that a young boy actually kept track of our Revolution. I read his reports and ended up staying awake all night with my thoughts. For six long years Congress has fretted and argued over starting our new government. I cannot count how many times I wanted to walk out while Massachusetts's representative bickered with Virginia's, or the southern ones opposed the northern ones. Somehow in all the politics, I'd lost the truth that I am a free American. Ben Johnston helped me find it again.

How easy it is to forget that we could not argue or disagree with King George—we could only obey or start a war. Amid our struggles to write a consti-

tution and form a government of the people, I also forgot the kind of men with whom I serve. They might quibble over a vote, but they would also march in snow and sleep in the cold to maintain our freedom.

I need—we need—these reports. I plan to give them to Congress's record clerk. Perhaps one day they will be in the library that Thomas Jefferson wants to start. But first, it is important that I add some final information about the men and women mentioned in them.

Francis Marion, the Swamp Fox, retired from military life. A couple of years ago he married a girl he has known since childhood. He is a farmer but still enjoys hunting and fishing in his swamps.

Benedict Arnold and Charles Lee were court-martialed. Arnold survived the war as a British officer and now lives in Canada. Lee was found guilty of disobeying a direct order and of disorderly retreat. He was suspended for a year. He died in 1782, angry at all.

The story of Deborah Sampson (alias Robert Shurtliff) made it into many newspapers, and she became well known. Though she is now married with two daughters and a son, she still gives talks about her life as a Revolutionary War soldier. Congress is talking of giving soldiers a pension. I suspect she will get eight dollars a month along with many others.

John Paul Jones ruffled a few political feathers and wasn't appointed by Congress to our new American navy. Instead he became a diplomat. A regular visitor to the French and Russian courts, he is a favorite of the royalty in both these countries. Later Congress did make a medal honoring his valor and brilliant services.

The Marquis de Lafayette testified at the court-martial of General Lee, but after the war he returned to France. There is much unrest in his country, and he speaks often of creating a government like ours. I fear things will not work out as he hoped. But whatever happens, he is loved in America. We'd welcome him back if he ever returned.

We never captured Mohawk Chief Joseph Brant. After the war he moved to Canada. Though our enemy, it cannot be denied he was a shrewd military man. The English were glad to have him.

As for Colonel George Clark, he's now known as the "Father of the Northwest Territories." Because of this man's efforts, we claimed the northwest in our peace treaty with England. Thomas Jefferson asked Colonel Clark to explore even farther west, but he refused since his health is poor. However, he has a younger brother named William, who fought beside him in the Revolution. Perhaps he'll make the journey.

Finally, a young soldier from the south named Andrew Jackson was mentioned in the reports. He is making a name for himself in the military. If we ever go to war again, I have little doubt he will be in the middle of it!

This completes these reports. Their importance to our young country cannot be measured. Just as they reminded me that my country is more than politics and petty squabbles, they can remind others. Liberty cannot be preserved without a general knowledge among our people. Let us always dare to think, to speak, and to act. Let us dare to follow the example of a general, a navy captain, a swamp fighter, an independent girl, and thousands of other patriots who struggled so mightily to ensure our freedom!

JOHN ADAMS

, and sent hither swarms of Officers to harrass our

— He has affected to render the Military independent

ledged by our laws; giving his Assent to their Acts

rent for any Murders which they should commit

r Consent: — For depriving us in many cases

h laws in a neighbouring Province, establishing

absolute rule into these Colonies: — For taki

un Legislatures, and declaring themselves inve

ing War against us. — He has plundered our

ies to compleat the works of death, desolation and ty

lized nation. — He has constrained our fellow

ves by their Hands. — He has excited domestic

s an undistinguished destruction of all ages, sexes a

answered by repeated injury. A Prince, whose cha

our British brethren. We have warned them from t

ion and settlement here. We have appealed to their n

vitably interrupt our connections and correspondenc